THE VEIL OF ASET

Tales of the Goddess

THE VEIL OF ASET: TALES OF THE GODDESS

ISBN-13 (soft cover): 978-1-951205-11-9

ISBN-13 (e-book): 978-1-951205-10-2

Publisher: Abracax House®
Author, Editor, Layout: Michael Coles
Original Artwork: Asim Hussain, Anna Dorzhieva

Authored, Edited and Designed in the United States of America.

Library of Congress Control Number: 9781951205119

10 9 8 7 6 5 4 3 2 1

"I AM ALL THAT HAS BEEN,
ALL THAT IS, AND
ALL THAT SHALL BE;
NO MORTAL HAS EVER
LIFTED MY VEIL."

TABLE OF CONTENTS

INTRODUCTION

"Aset, Awaken within our hearts. Open the star chamber that we may guide our transformation into Heru."

N the great pantheon of Kemetic gods and goddesses, none was more beloved than the Great Goddess Aset, known to the Greeks as *Isis*. The tales of her exploits are numerous and are key to understanding the Ancestors' faith.

So, what made her so popular? Perhaps it was the way she took care of the common people. We know that she is credited with teaching the women of Kemet how to brew beer, bake bread, weave cloth, and use healing magic, for instance. She is the prototype for Mother Nature, the divine protector who helped escort the dead to the Western Lands, and the healer of the sick and injured.

Maybe the people loved her because of her fascinating stories. She was the Great Sorceress, she who was called "cleverer than a million gods". She was persistent, and never took "no" for an answer. The Goddess knew what she wanted, and she was willing to use all her wisdom and great powers to get it. It was her sheer force of will that forced Amun-Ra to leave the earth, placed her husband and son successively on the throne, and rescued both from the icy grip of death.

I would argue, however, that Aset was the most popular deity because she was the most *human* deity.

No doubt the Ancestors could relate to Aset's pain and suffering, just as we can today. She experienced more tragedy than any god or goddess before her, and she dealt with her pain in very human ways. When her husband was unfaithful and her sister betrayed her, her anger and disappointment were justified and understandable. When her husband was murdered, and his body scattered over the world, her grief was palpable. People could understand her pain, pain that literally stopped the sun in its tracks, when her son died.

Perhaps more importantly though, Aset taught people compassion. Though she was angry at her husband's disloyalty, she rescued and adopted his illegitimate love-child, raising him as her own. When Aset's scorpions killed the son of the woman who scorned her, the Goddess took pity on the woman and raised her son from the dead. And when that same woman gave all her earthly possessions to Aset, the Goddess gifted it all to the poor woman who treated her with proper dignity and respect.

In her role as Divine Mother, the Goddess provided a perfect role model for raising children. She taught her son Heru to properly venerate the gods, helped him find his purpose, and used all her powers to fight side-by-side with him to help him succeed in his battles.

In this book, we have compiled several tales of the Goddess. They have been placed in approximate chronological order, but they are from different sources, and potentially different cults, making some of them a little harder to pin down precisely. For instance, the story "The Scorpions of Aset" takes place after the murder of Ausar and the Divine Conception, but before Heru's birth. In some traditions, the story takes place after the birth of Heru, making this particular story a little harder to place exactly in the timeline. Rest assured we've put a lot of effort into making sure the timeline and other details are coherent in the form presented.

In other cases, there are may be multiple contradictory stories, as in the tale "Set Takes Heru's Eyes". In an alternate telling of the tale, Set turns himself into a fierce black pig and shoots fire from his snout to burn Heru's eye. In this book we have chosen to use the story from the *Contendings of Heru and Set*, because it fits with the overall story arc of this book better. (The alternate story of Set turning into a pig is contained in the *The Kemetic Tarot: Veil of Aset Edition* companion book).

In the "Final Contest", there are multiple alternate endings as well. In the Memphis Theogony, for instance, the Creator God Ptah calls upon the Earth God Geb and orders him to pass judgement. In other traditions, Amun-Ra orders Aset to bind Set and bring him before the Council as her prisoner. Amun-Ra then passes judgement on him. We have combined these two traditions in this story, as they need not be contradictory.

Finally, in other tellings of the great battles between Heru and Set, Re-Horakhty (the "Lord-of-the-Boundary"), is the "Master of the Universe", and he manages the trial of Heru and Set. In many instances, alternate titles and names are used for Re-Horakhty throughout the original texts. To simplify things, we've simply gone with Amun-Ra for consistency instead of using several alternate titles and names.

THE KNOT OF ASET

HE Knot of Aset ("Knot of Isis"), or *tjet*, is a protective amulet resembling a person with arms by its side, facing downward. Traditionally, the tjet could be made with a variety of stones. Red jasper, referenced in *The Egyptian Book of Coming Forth By Day*, was one of the most popular varieties. The red jasper stone is commonly knows as a stone of nurturing, and is traditionally associated with emotional stamina, inner strength, protection, courage, balance, relaxation, and calm.

The tjet protective amulet included in the Kemetic Tarot: Veil of Aset Edition is made of red jasper, primarily because of its protective properties.

Chapter 156 of *The Egyptian Book of Coming Forth By Day* includes the following spell, designed to imbue the tjet amulet with the protective power of Aset:

"By the blood of Aset; by the power of Aset; by the magic of Aset: This amulet protects the Great One and shall drive away any who would do wrong against her (or him)."

This chapter is said over a tjet made of red jasper, which has been washed with rose water in a bowl made of sycamore wood.

The amulet was believed to provide protection to both the living in the mundane world and the traveler through the duat (the land of the dead.) The body of she (or he) who performs this ritual shall be protected by the power of Aset; and Heru, son of Aset, shall rejoice when he greets her (or him). No path shall be hidden from her (or him), and one side of her (or him) shall be towards the sky and the other side towards the earth. A true matter: you shall let no one see this amulet in your hand, for there is nothing equal to it.

THE BIRTH OF ASET

A S is well-known, Amun-Ra first created himself and pulled himself out of the watery abyss of Nun. Amun-Ra delegated to the primordial gods the tasks of defining rules by which the world would function, such as the god Ḥeḥ, who defined the length of the year as 360 days.

Standing on Ben-Ben, the primordial mound he had established in the middle of the watery abyss, Amun-Ra spat, and in so doing, created two children for himself: Shu, god of wind, and Tefnut, goddess of moisture. Shu and Tefnut paired and had children of their own: Geb, god of earth, and Nut, goddess of the sky.

Amun-Ra then fashioned the sun and the moon, the stars and the cosmos, and the fish and the animals. Finally, he created man and woman. And Amun-Ra lived on the earth among his creation as their divine ruler, during a golden age.

Now it came to pass that Wadjet, the divine uraeus Eye of Ra, whispered a prophecy into Amun-Ra's ear, saying, "Your great-grandson shall depose you and replace you as divine ruler of the world."

Amun-Ra pondered this revelation and decided no one would ever replace him on the Throne of the Two

Lands. So, the grand creator cursed his granddaughter, Nut, with the following words: "I place this curse on my grand-daughter Nut, that she shall not bear any children on any day or night of the year. So says Amun-Ra."

Now Geb and Nut were inseparable, and Geb had impregnated Nut with five of his children. The curse of Amun-Ra, however, prevented her from giving birth, and her agony increased as the children grew in her womb.

In desperation, Nut turned to the wisest of all the gods, Tehuti, for help. The god of wisdom considered her situation, and he searched all the magical texts of his great library for a method of reversing the curse of Amun-Ra. He soon discovered, however, that the curse of Amun-Ra is ir-reversible and none can break it.

As Tehuti carefully considered the words of Amun-Ra's curse, "…she shall not bear any children on any day or night of the year", he suddenly realized how to defeat it.

So Tehuti put his plan into action, by calling upon the young moon god Khonsu. Now the Moon God was an avid collector of magic and an insatiable gambler, so Khonsu pro-posed a wager with him: they would bet a portion of their power on a game of senet. If Khonsu won, Tehuti would give the moon god a portion of his magical powers and am-ulets. If the Tehuti won, Khonsu would give the god of wis-dom a portion of his moonlight.

Khonsu agreed and the two sat down to play the game. The game lasted several days, but in the end, Tehuti's intricate knowledge of strategy and his great wisdom and ex-perience overpowered Khonsu's reckless playing style. In the end, Khonsu had to give Tehuti a 1/72 portion of his power.

To this day, the moon wanes throughout the month as it loses power and waxes as it recovers.

Tehuti then used the moonlight he had acquired from Khonsu to extend the year by five days, so that instead of 360 days, the year would be 365 days in length.

During the extra five days, which were not part of the year, Nut was able to give birth to her five children. And on each of the days, she gave birth to one of her divine children: Ausar, Heru the Elder, Set, Aset, and Nebet-Het.

When Amun-Ra heard that his grand-daughter had given birth, he was furious at her. As punishment, he ordered Nut's father, Shu, to stand on Geb and hold Nut up with his hands, permanently separating the lovers for all time.

And Nut never had any regrets, for she loved her children exceedingly.

AMUN-RA'S SECRET NAME

Y the time Aset reached adulthood, she had become a favorite of the gods. The moon god Khonsu and the god of wisdom Tehuti both spent much of their time teaching her the ways of Heka (magic) and how to use magical words of power. Under the divine tutelage of the gods, Aset became a renowned sorceress throughout the world.

One day, Aset heard the cries of the people of the land of Kemet. The land was parched, the crops were burning, and nothing could grow. The great drought was starving the people.

As she looked over the kingdom, Aset suddenly realized why the land was scorched – it was Amun-Ra. Amun-Ra's cosmic power was exceedingly great, and it was burning up his creation. So Aset devised a plan.

Aset acquired a measure of Amun-Ra's spittle, which she mixed with dirt to create a poisonous viper of the mud mixture. Then she endowed the viper with life and set it loose in Amun-Ra's garden.

As all the gods and mortals knew, Amun-Ra went for a walk each morning in his divine garden, so he could review his creation. The next morning, when the creator god walked in his garden, Aset's poisonous viper bit him upon his heel.

Amun-Ra used a word of power to order the poisonous venom to leave his body. But the venom would not leave.

Intrigued, the creator god used another word of power to purge his body of the viper's poison. But the poison was stubborn and stayed within his body. After a while, Amun-Ra retired to his throne and pondered these wonders.

Over the course of many days, Amun-Ra's health began failing because of the viper's poison. His jaws chattered, his lips trembled, and he even lost the power of speech for a short time; never had he suffered such pain. Khonsu was called to work his magic, but the moon god could not expunge the poison from Amun-Ra's body. Hathor was then called, but for all her healing powers, she could not remove the poison either. Tehuti was called upon, but he could find no cure in his great library. Finally, Aset was requested to assist the ailing creator god.

After examining Amun-Ra, Aset said she could cure him with a magic spell, but he must reveal his secret name to her in order to make the spell work. So Amun-Ra said, "My names are many: I am the Hidden One, Giver of Life, Grandest Creator, the Ram of the West, Ra Who Is the Heru of the Horizons, and the Complete One."

Aset cast her spell using the names Amun-Ra had given her, but to no effect. She said to him again, "Grand Creator, the only way I can cast the venom from your body is if you tell me your secret name."

Amun-Ra then told her, "I am Khepera in the morning; I am Ra at midday; and I am Atum at dusk."

Aset again cast her spell using these names, but they again failed to extract the poison from Amun-Ra's body. "O great Amun-Ra," she said to the creator god, "tease me no more! But tell me your secret name that I might finally cure you of this affliction!"

Amun-Ra pondered Aset's request, and as his health was failing fast, finally he decided to reveal his secret name to the goddess. "Listen with your heart," he whispered to her.

Amun-Ra then spoke his secret name directly from his heart to the heart of Aset. Suddenly the goddess felt a surge of electricity as the creator god's secret name imbued her with his great power.

Aset began to cast her spell using Amun-Ra's secret name, but she suddenly stopped. "Amun-Ra," she said to him, "everywhere you walk in the kingdom, your cosmic power burns the crops and scorches the land. Your power cannot be resisted by the fragility of your creation. Your subjects cry out in pain and agony, from the sheer heat."

"I will finish my spell, and cure you of this poison," Aset continued, "but only if you will leave the earth so that your own creation might flourish, and appoint my husband Ausar as ruler so the people will have a benevolent and wise god to lead them."

Amun-Ra's first reaction was anger. "You insolent fool! How dare you attempt to extort the greatest of the gods!" he shouted.

But even as he pondered Aset's wise words, he listened closely to the cries of his subjects. It became clear to him that she was right. His own cosmic power was destroying his very creation and killing his people.

"Very well," the creator god said, at last. "After you draw this viper's venom from my body, I shall appoint your husband Ausar as ruler of the world, and I shall leave the earth so that my creation might continue. As Amun-Ra has said it, so let it be done."

And with that unbreakable divine oath spoken, Aset finished her spell, saying "Flow, poison, come forth from Amun-Ra. Eye of Heru, come forth from Amun-Ra and shine outside his mouth. It is I, Aset, who works, and I have made the poison to fall on the ground. Verily the name of the great god is taken from him, Amun-Ra shall live and the poison shall die; if the poison live Amun-Ra shall die."

And with this infallible spell, used in cases of poisoning, the bite of the venomous reptile was rendered harmless. The poison was driven from Amun-Ra's body.

The creator god immediately recovered, and true to his word, he called the gods and the people together, and formally appointed his great-grandson Ausar as ruler of the world. He then charged Tehuti with teaching the mortals *Weret-Hekau*, the words of magic, which would protect them from poisons and afflictions which might befall them.

To fulfill his pledge, Amun-Ra called upon the goddess Hathor, and in the form of a cow, she carried him to the Atet, his great barque in the heavens, which he uses to cross the sky every day and the underworld of the duat each night.

THE BETRAYAL OF ASET

NCE Ausar became ruler of the world, he looked upon Aset and decided to take her as his wife. They resided in a royal palace in the fertile lands of Kemet, where they ruled with benevolence and wisdom. Ausar taught his people to cultivate and improve the fruits of the earth, and he gave them a body of laws to enforce justice. He also taught them how to show reverence and worship the gods. And the people of Kemet prospered.

Ausar's brother Set took the goddess Nebet-Het as his consort and Set and Nebet-Het were sent away from Kemet by Amun-Ra to rule the Deshret. Angry at his exile to the red lands, Set was merciless and cruel to his subjects. Nebet-Het found no joy in being married to the god Set, and lived in constant fear of his terrible temper. One day she decided to leave the infertile red lands and live with her sister Aset in the fertile black lands of Kemet.

Aset welcomed her sister Nebet-Het with open arms and provided her a royal suite and a full staff of handmaidens to see to her every need. And Nebet-Het and Aset were happy to be in each other's company.

But jealousy can be a dangerous emotion. As Nebet-Het watched the love her sister Aset shared with her husband Ausar, she grew resentful that she had never experienced such true love with her own husband. And as she became ever more envious, she imagined how much better her life would be if she could but take her sister's place. And from these seeds of envy, planted deep within Nebet-Het's heart, she began to grow a plan to experience her sister's bliss.

Late one night while Aset was away from the palace, Nebet-Het used her words of power to assume her sister's form. It was in this guise that she sneaked into the pharaoh's bed chamber late that night. Believing his beloved Aset had returned from her travels, Ausar kissed the imposter. Excited at the embrace of this man who believed she was his beloved, Nebet-Het aroused Ausar and straddled his naked body. She spent the night seducing the pharaoh in his own bed.

Once their intimate dalliance was complete, Ausar fell fast asleep. Nebet-Het left a garland of sweet melilote, her favorite flower, at his bedside. Then she sneaked out as the pharaoh slept.

When Aset returned home from her long journey, she noticed the garland, made of sweet melilote, in the bed chamber of her husband Ausar; and she grew suspicious.

When the queen confronted Nebet-Het, and her sister admitted to the tryst with Ausar. Nebet-Het told Aset she had tricked the pharaoh into making love to her, and he was blameless. She begged the queen for mercy, and told her she had been impregnated by the pharaoh. "I abandoned the baby in the reeds of the marshlands at night," she admitted to Aset.

Aset immediately grabbed her sister by the arm and pulled her along, crying, "Take me there, now!"

Shocked, Nebet-Het complied. She led her sister to the marsh where the abandoned baby lay in a small bed of reeds. Aset picked up the infant and said to it, "I give to you the name Anpu, meaning 'the Royal Child'. As Ausar has given me no child to care for, I swear I shall raise you as my own."

Aset then carried Anpu back to Kemet, where she kept her oath and raised the baby god as if he was her own son. Aset forgave both her sister Nebet-Het and her husband Ausar; and she never held any ill will toward either from that day onward.

THE SEARCH FOR AUSAR

HE reign of Ausar was benefi-cent. During his rule, the land prospered and the people of Ke-met were satisfied. But Ausar's brother Set became jealous of his brother's power and his popular-ity among his subjects. And it came to pass that through trick-ery and deceit, Set murdered his brother Ausar and had the phar-aoh's body encased in a sealed box and thrown into the Nile, to be carried out to sea.

He then took for himself the Throne of the Two Lands and assumed the title of pharaoh of Kemet. And the people were outraged at the murder of their good pharaoh, and they were distressed at the harsh rule of Set. And a dark-ness covered the land, as even the gods were alarmed at Set's nefarious actions.

When the pharaoh's wife Aset and her sister Nebet-Het heard of Ausar's murder, they ran to the Nile and began wailing and weeping for the dead pharaoh. The divine sisters mourned together for days, crying so much that the people believed the yearly inundation was due to their mournful tears. That day, the sisters made a vow to search the world for Ausar's body, that they might return him to his homeland and give him the funeral rites required by the gods.

The sister goddesses walked the length of the Nile, asking children who were playing on the shore whether they had seen the pharaoh's body floating downstream. As they gathered what little information they could from the children, Aset placed her divine blessing on each and every child they encountered.

When the sisters reached the delta where the Nile pours forth into the sea, they took the shape of birds and split up, that they might continue searching from the skies high above. While searching the land of Phoenicia, word came to Aset's ear of a miraculous tamarisk tree—the largest ever seen—that had suddenly appeared in the city of Byblos. Aset found out the tree had been cut down by Melcander, the king of Byblos, to be used as a pillar in his newly-constructed palace.

Upon hearing of this great tree, Aset decided to investigate further. But first, she decided to rest at the seashore. Aset took the form of an old woman and sat upon the shore, where fair maidens of Queen Astarte came to bathe in the moonlit waters. When the maidens came out of the waters, the Goddess taught them to plait their hair, and to weave fragrant flowers and leaves into it, in a style which had never before been done.

As the maidens returned to the palace, the Queen marveled at their hair, and at the strange and wonderful scent of perfume that clung to them. The maidens told the Queen about the kindly old woman who sat on the shore, and the Queen sent for her.

When Aset arrived at the palace, Queen Astarte was so impressed by this extraordinary Kemetic woman that she offered her a position in the palace, caring for her children. Aset accepted and started to work immediately.

Now one of the Queen's children, a baby named Dictys, was ailing. Aset nursed the baby on her finger, so that soon he was fully recovered and healthy. The Goddess became exceedingly fond of this child, and decided to grant him immortality. To do this, she cast a spell and placed him over the fire to burn away his mortal parts, even as she flew around the room in the shape of a sparrow.

The Queen spied the ritual through a crack in the door and became alarmed. She rushed into the room with a loud cry and grabbed her son from the fire, breaking the spell.

"Foolish mortal woman!" Aset rebuked the Queen as she returned to her own glorious form. "If you had left your son to my care, I would have burned away all that is mortal within him and made him an immortal Neteru god!"

At these words, spoken by the divine goddess in her true form, the Queen went into a state of awe and terror.

19

Aset told the Queen her son's immortality was now forfeit, because of her irreverence.

Queen Astarte ordered her servants to bring the King. As he entered the divine presence of Aset, he likewise dropped to his knees and begged the goddess for forgiveness. The King then offered the goddess all the treasures of the kingdom, lest the royal couple offend her a second time.

But Aset requested only the great tamarisk pillar holding up the roof of the palace, for she had confirmed it sprouted around and enveloped the chest holding the body of her beloved husband Ausar.

The King ordered the pillar be given to Aset immediately, and with a word of power, the goddess split the great pillar in two. She carefully removed the chest holding Ausar's body and carried it back to Kemet, where she planned to give the pharaoh a proper funeral.

THE DIVINE CONCEPTION OF HERU

ETURNING from Byblos with the casket of her beloved husband Ausar, the goddess Aset decided to hide his body among the reeds of the Nile until she could properly embalm the pharaoh and give him proper funeral rites.

While Aset was away from the kingdom searching for Ausar's body, however, Set had established a network of spies throughout the land. One of his many spies saw Aset hiding the pharaoh's sarcophagus in the reeds of the Nile, and he reported this back to Set. Set, the usurper to the Throne of the Two Lands, then sent his men to the Nile to retrieve his brother's body.

Once he had possession of the pharaoh's body, Set defiled it and ripped it into 14 pieces. He flung the body parts all over the world, including Ausar's phallus, which was swallowed by a medjed (elephant fish), which is considered sacred to this day.

When Aset found out what Set had done to the body of her beloved, she turned herself into a hawk and searched the world, recovering the body pieces one by one. Once she had recovered all the far-flung parts of her lover's body, Aset returned them to Kemet, where she enlisted the aid of Anpu to mummify the royal corpse.

Using linen strips and magic, Aset, Anpu, Nebet-Het, and Tehuti worked together to properly preserve the body of Ausar. And after his body was whole again, Aset used words of power to impregnate herself with her murdered lover's seed.

And so was it written in the scriptures: "Your sister Aset acted as a protectress to you. She drove away your enemies, she averted seasons of calamity from you, she recited the words of power with the magic of her mouth, being skilled of tongue and never halting for a word, being perfect in command and word.

"Aset the sorceress avenged her brother. She went about seeking for him untiringly. She flew round and round over the earth uttering wailing cries of grief, and she did not alight on the ground until she had found him. She made light come forth from her feathers, she made air come into being by means of her two wings, and she cried out the death cries for her brother. She made to rise up the helpless members of him whose heart was at rest, she drew from him his essence, and she made therefrom an heir."

THE SCORPIONS OF ASET

AM Aset, Speaker of Spells, the Great Goddess, Mistress of Magic, Keeper of the Words of Power. I am known by many names, but you may call me Aset.

I was imprisoned by my brother Set in the Deshret, in a prison which was shielded from the workings of my magic. Set desired that I should marry him to validate his claim to the Throne of the Two Lands, but I steadfastly refused.

I was, at the time, pregnant with the son of my husband, the great god Ausar. My son would be named Heru, rightful heir to the Throne of Two Lands. I had to hide my pregnancy from my captor, lest he decide to harm me or my child; but I knew I would not be able to hide my belly forever.

In my state of greatest distress, I called out to the gods for help. It was Tehuti, the twice great, who came to me. He told me he would blind Set's guards as Amun-Ra descended on the Western horizon, and at that moment I could escape the prison of Set.

That evening, the guards were blinded by the brilliance of the setting sun, just as Tehuti had promised. I ran out of my prison cell, and seven scorpions traveled with me: Petet, Thetet, and Matet cleared the path before me; Mestet and Mestetef walked beside me; and Tefen and Befen guarded the road behind.

Once we were far from Set's prison, I called to the scorpions. My words rang through the air as I commanded them, "Do not know 'the Black One' and do not greet 'the Red One'. Do not distinguish the nobles from the commoners. Look neither at children nor at any small and helpless creature."

And I continued my journey until we approached the swamps and marshes of the North Country. As we came near the houses of the marsh people, a noblewoman named Glory stood in her doorway, watching as I came near. I walked up to her to inquire of the noble lady that I might rest in her house. But the woman slammed the door in my face, before I could utter the words.

I walked along a bit further and a poor woman of the marsh opened her door to me, and invited me in for a respite. Though her provisions were meager, she offered me the best food and drink in her house.

Now the seven scorpions remained outside, guarding the poor woman's house as I rested. They were angered that the noblewoman had disrespected their mistress so. They plotted together, and decided to combine their poison, which they placed upon the boldest of their members, the scorpion Tefen. This instantly gave Tefen a sting of seven-fold power.

Tefen silently returned to the house of the noble-woman, whose name was Glory; the same woman who had closed her door against me. The door was still shut, but there was a narrow opening between the door and the threshold. It was through this narrow space that Tefen entered the house and stung the son of the noblewoman with his seven-fold powerful sting. Tefen's sting was so fierce and burning that the woman's son died instantly, and a fire broke out in her house.

The noblewoman Glory wailed and lamented, but no man came to her aid. At last, the heavens opened up and poured water upon her house—a great marvel indeed, for it was not yet the inundation season.

The noblewoman continued to mourn and grieve in the middle of the road, even as she cradled the lifeless body of her son in her arms. My heart swelled with sorrow for the wailing woman, so I went outside to her. As I approached the noblewoman, she looked up at me, and I could see in her eyes that her heart was full of regret for having turned me away in my time of need.

And I, Aset, Mistress of Magic, whose voice can awaken the dead, called aloud the Words of Power—words that even the dead can hear. And I laid my arms upon the child that I might bring back Life to the Lifeless body. I spoke the magic words of Weret-Hekau to the poison of Tefen: "O poison of Tefen, come out of him and fall upon the ground! Poison of Befen, advance not, penetrate no further, come out of him and fall upon the ground! For I am Aset, the Great Enchantress, the Speaker of Spells. Fall down, O poison of Mestet! Hasten not, poison of Mestetef! Rise not, poison of Petet and Thetet! Approach not, poison of Matet! For I am Aset, the Great Enchantress, Speaker of Spells. The child shall live, the poison shall die! As Heru is strong and well for me, his mother, so shall this child be strong and well for his mother!"

Then the child recovered, the fire was quenched, and the rain from the heavens ceased. And the noblewoman Glory brought all her wealth—her bracelets, necklaces, gold and silver jewelry—to the house of the poor woman, and she laid them at my feet in a token of repentance for her sin.

I graciously accepted her offerings, and then I gave them all to the poor woman who had offered me her hospitality, though I was a stranger to her. And the noblewoman's wealth filled the poor woman's entire home.

To this day, men make dough of wheat-flour kneaded with salt and lay it upon the wound made by the sting of a scorpion; and over this they recite the Words of Power which I myself recited over the child of the noblewoman.

For I am Aset, Speaker of Spells, the Great Goddess, Mistress of Magic, and Keeper of the Words of Power.

THE DEATH AND RESURRECTION
OF HERU

HEN Aset finally gave birth to Heru, the brutal god Set still ruled over Kemet. Aset knew that she could not let word of Heru's birth reach Set's ear, lest he send his assassins for the true heir to the Throne of the Two Lands. So the Goddess raised her son in hiding, in the northern marshlands, among the reeds.

Now Heru grew in size and stature, until he towered over other men. And Aset taught him what she knew of heka magic, nature, fighting, and his destiny to avenge his father and battle his uncle Set for rule over the Two Lands.

But news of Heru's birth could not be kept from Set's spies forever. One day, while Aset was performing a religious ceremony in honor of Ausar at a temple, Set sent forth the terrible scorpion Uhat to assassinate young Heru. Uhat discovered the hiding place of Heru, and it stung and killed the son of Ausar. Upon her return to the marshlands, Aset burst forth in lamentations, and the peoples of the marshlands cried with her.

Aset held the dead body of her son high in the air as she cried out to the gods, "Heru is bitten! The heir of heaven, the son of Ausar, the child of the gods, he who is wholly fair, is bitten! He whose wants I provided; he who is destined to avenge his father, is bitten! He for whom I cared and suffered even as I fashioned him in my womb, is bitten! He whom I tended so that I might gaze upon him, is bitten! He whose life I prayed for is bitten! Calamity has overtaken the child, and he has perished!"

As Aset wept for the loss of her divine son, her sister Nebet-Het wept with her. The scorpion goddess Serqet approached the sisters from the reeds and advised the goddesses to pray to heaven for help. And together they prayed, "We pray that the sailors in the Mesket, the solar barque of Amun-Ra, cease their rowing! For the barque cannot move forward while Heru lies dead!"

And their voices reached the Mesket, and the great disc ceased moving, and it came to a standstill. Tehuti, he who is equipped with words of power and all manner of spells, descended from the Mesket, and he brought with him the great command of maa-kheru, the true voice, which compels all gods, spirits, mortals, and every thing—animate and inanimate—in heaven and on earth.

Then Tehuti came to Aset and told her that no harm could have happened to Heru, for he was under the protection of the Mesket; but his words brought Aset no comfort. Even as she acknowledged the greatness of the cosmic designs, she complained of the delay. "What is the good of all your spells, incantations, heka, and the command of maakheru if Heru is to perish by the poison of a scorpion?"

Tehuti turned to Aset and Nebet-Het, and he assured them that Heru was under the protection of the Dweller in the Disc, the Great Dwarf, the Mighty Ram, the Great Hawk, the Holy Scarab, the Hidden One, and the Divine Bennu. "Fear not," he said to them, "for I have come from heaven to heal the child for his mother."

He then pronounced the great spell which restored Heru to life. And with his words of power, Tehuti transferred the fluid of life to Heru, and the scorpion's poison flowed out of the child god, and he breathed and lived once more.

After Heru recovered, Tehuti spoke to Aset, telling her that he would hereafter personally act as Heru's advocate in the Hall of Two Truths, and that he would make all accusations brought against Heru recoil back on the accusers. Further, he granted Heru the power to repulse the attacks made on him by gods from above or demons from below, to ensure his succession to the Throne of Geb.

He carefully explained Aset's role in restoring Heru's life, saying, "It is the words of power of the mother which have lifted up his fact; and they shall enable him to travel wherever he pleases. They shall put fear into the powers above; I, myself, hasten to obey them."

Thus, it was stated plainly to the goddess's ear that Heru's destiny hinged on Aset's words of power, she who made the sun stand still and caused the dead to be raised.

When all was done, Tehuti returned to the Mesket and the solar barque continued on its daily journey across the sky.

The gods in the heavens, who were distraught at the death of Heru, were joyful once more, and they sang songs of joy at the news of his recovery.

The Trial of Heru and Set

NE night Ausar appeared to his son Heru in a dream. The ghost of Ausar urged his son to avenge him and overthrow the pretender to the throne, Set. Upon receiving this sign from his father, Heru gathered his army and went forth to battle Set.

The war between Heru's and Set's armies ravaged the Two Kingdoms for many years, and at long last, Set the usurper was driven out of Kemet.

It was then that Amun-Ra ordered Tehuti to descend from the heavens and heal the wounds of both Heru and Set. As soon as he was healed of his injuries, however, Set demanded an audience with the Council of the Gods to present his claims. Amun-Ra considered Set's demand, and he agreed. The Creator God assembled the Great Council to hear the pleadings of both Heru and Set. And it came to pass that the two mighty princes stood before the Council of the Gods to argue their cases.

Shu, son of Amun-Ra, spoke first: "All justice is powerful. Give the kingly office to Heru."

Tehuti, god of wisdom, proclaimed his agreement with Shu, saying, "Yes! This is a million times right!"

Aset rejoiced and gave a great cry of joy. She called upon the North Wind to blow Westward to whisper the good news to Ausar.

Then Amun-Ra, the Creator God, questioned the Council: "Under whose authority do you take such bold action?"

And the Council responded, "The prince has taken the royal name of Heru, and they have set the Hedjet White Crown upon his head."

Amun-Ra contemplated the words of the Great Council, but he was angry with them.

Then Set said, "Let Heru be cast forth with me, that I may defeat him in a trial in the presence of the Great Council."

But Tehuti replied, "That will not tell us who is the guilty one here. Should the office of Ausar be given to his brother, while his son Heru yet lives?"

Upon hearing this, Amun-Ra grew exceedingly angry, for it was his wish to give the kingly office to Set, the son of Nut, because of his great strength.

Then Anhur, the god of war, uttered a great cry before the Council, asking them "What are we to do?!"

With that, Amun-Ra said: "Let Banebdjed, the great living ram-god, be summoned to pronounce judgement upon these two striplings."

So Banebdjeb, the great god who dwells in Setit, and the great god Ptah, were both brought before Amun-Ra. And the Creator God said to them, "Pronounce judgement upon these two striplings, and stop them from fighting every day and destroying the Two Kingdoms."

Banebdjeb, the great god, surveyed the situation and used the art of diplomacy when he answered the Council. He said to the tribunal, "Let us not take action in our ignorance. Rather, send a letter to the primordial goddess Neith the mighty, the mother of gods. What she decrees, so shall we do."

The Council responded to Banbdjeb: "Judgement was made between them in the primordial times in the Hall of Two Truths."

Then Tehuti was asked by Amun-Ra to send a letter to Neith the mighty, mother of gods. Tehuti immediately accepted the commission, responding: "I will do it, truly I will do it!"

Tehuti composed the letter to the goddess Neith, asking her to pronounce judgement on Heru and Set. Upon receiving Tehuti's letter, Neith, the mother of gods, advised the Council of the Gods that they should avoid engaging in great acts of wickedness, but rather they should immediately give Heru the Hedjet White Crown and seat him on the Throne of the Two Lands. She also ruled that Amun-Ra should double Set's possessions, and give him his two daughters, Anat and Astarte.

When the letter of Neith, the mother of gods, reached the Council, Tehuti read it aloud to them. Neith's response angered Amun-Ra, and he directed his rage at Heru, saying: "You are feeble in your limbs, and this kingly office is too great for you! You are but a stripling with a bad taste in your mouth!"

And Anhur grew angry a million times over, and the entire Council grew angry with him. The god Baba rose up and shouted at Amun-Ra: "Your shrine is empty!"

Amun-Ra was aggrieved at this taunt, and he laid upon his back, his heart sore. The Council went forth and cried before the face of the god Baba, and they said to him, "Get out! This crime you have done is exceedingly great!"

Then the members of the Council went to their tents to contemplate all that had happened that day.

Meanwhile, the Creator God spent an entire day lying on his back, alone in his garden, with a heavy heart. After a long while, Hathor, the lady of the southern sycamore, stood before her father Amun-Ra and uncovered her nakedness before his face. And the Creator God laughed at her.

Thereupon, Amun-Ra rose up and rejoined the Great Council. He commanded both Heru and Set to defend their claims.

Set began: "I am Set, greatest of the Pesedjet, the Great Council of Nine Gods. I slay the enemy of Amun-Ra daily, as I sit in the front of the Barque of Millions of Years, and no other god is able to do this. I am entitled to the office of Ausar."

The Great Council considered Set's words and they responded by saying, "Set, the son of Nut, is in the right."

Tehuti and Anhur cried aloud, saying, "Shall the office be given to a brother on the side of the mother, while a son of the body is yet alive?!"

And Banebdjed responded, saying, "Shall the office be given to a young stripling, while Set, his elder brother, is yet alive?"

The Council cried aloud before the face of Amun-Ra, and they said to him, "What are these words that you have spoken, which are not worthy to be heard?"

Then spoke Heru, son of Aset, "This is no good, truly, that I should be cheated in the presence of the Council of Gods, and that the office of my father Ausar should be taken away from me."

Aset grew angry with the Great Council, and she made an oath in their presence: "As my mother, the goddess Neith, lives; and as Ptah-tanen, high of plumes, curber of the horns of gods, lives, these words shall be placed before Atum, the mighty prince who is in Heliopolis, and likewise before Khepera who dwells in his barque."

The Council responded to her, "Do not be vexed. His rights shall be given unto him who is in the right, and all that which you have said shall be done."

And Set, son of Nut, was angry with the Council for speaking such kind words to Aset. He said to them: "I will take my heavy scepter and I will kill one of you each day."

Then he made an oath to Amun-Ra, saying, "I will not participate in this tribunal while Aset stands in its midst."

After Amun-Ra pondered Set's words, he ordered the Council of Gods to cross the river to Island-in-the-Middle. To the ferryman, Nemty, Amun-Ra said, "Do not ferry across any woman in the form of Aset."

ASET AND THE FERRYMAN

FTER Amun-Ra ordered the Great Council of the Gods to cross the river to Island-in-the-Middle, he ordered Nemty the ferryman to refuse passage to any woman who looked like Aset. The Council then crossed the river and arrived at Island-in-the-Middle, where they sat down and ate bread.

Meanwhile, Aset changed herself into the form of an old woman and approached Nemty, who was sitting in his boat. She spoke to the ferryman, asking him to ferry her across to Island-in-the-Middle, so that she might carry a jar of flour to her hungry son, who was watching after some cattle.

Nemty spoke to her, saying, "I was told not to ferry across any woman."

Aset, in the form of the old woman, said, "Were you ordered not to ferry women across because of Aset?"

Nemty's curiosity grew, so he asked the old woman, "What would you give me, if I ferried you across to Island-in-the-Middle?"

Aset then offered the ferryman her loaf of bread in exchange for passage to Island-in-the-Middle.

"Should I risk ferrying you across—when I've been ordered not to ferry any woman across—for the sake of a loaf of bread?" Nemty snapped at her.

Aset then offered him the ring of gold on her finger. "Let me have the ring of gold," he said.

Aset gave him the ring of gold and he ferried her across the river to Island-in-the-Middle. As she walked through the forest, the Goddess saw the Council sitting and eating bread in the presence of Amun-Ra in his garden.

Aset uttered a magical spell to convert herself into a fair maiden, unlike any other ever seen in the Two Lands. Then she approached the Great Council. When Set saw her, he immediately fell in love with her, and he stood up exclaiming, "I am here with you, fair maiden! What ails you?"

And she spoke to him, saying, "Nay, my great lord! As for me, I was the wife of a cattle herdsman, and I bore unto him a male child. But, lo, my husband died and the stripling came to look after the cattle of his father.

"But one day, a foreigner came, and he made his home in my cowshed, and he threatened my son, saying, 'I will beat you and take away your father's cattle, and I will throw you out!'

"But I wish only that you would be my son's champion."

And Set said to her, "Shall the cattle be given to the foreigner while the son of the good man is alive? I shall beat the stranger's face with a stick, and he shall be thrown out, and your son will be set in the place of his father."

Aset immediately changed herself into the form of a kite, and flew up and perched herself on the top of an acacia tree. And she called down to Set, saying, "Weep for yourself; your own mouth has said it; it is your own cleverness which judges you. What ails you now?"

Set stood weeping after Aset had beguiled him so. Amun-Ra then spoke to him: "Look at you now—you've passed judgement upon yourself. What ails you now?"

And Set quickly changed the subject, by saying, "Bring Nemty, the ferryman, and inflict on him a great punishment for defying the order of Amun-Ra and ferrying a woman across."

Upon hearing these words, the Council brought Nemty before them and removed the soles of his feet. And Nemty swore off gold in the presence of the tribunal, saying, "Gold has made me an abomination for my city."

The Contendings of
Heru and Set

HORTLY after punishing the ferryman Nemty for carrying Aset across the river, the Council crossed over to the Western Tract, where they sat down on the mountain. At evening time, Amun-Ra said to them, "What are you doing still sitting here? As for these two striplings, you will cause them to end their lives in this tribunal! I command you to set the Hedjet White Crown upon the head of Heru and promote him to the place of his father Ausar."

Upon hearing this, Set was angered. And the Council asked Set, "Why are you angry? Are we to not do what Amun-Ra, lord of the Two Lands in Heliopolis has commanded?"

Thereupon they set the Hedjet White Crown on the head of Heru, son of Aset. And Set cried aloud before the Council: "Shall the office be given to my little brother while I, the older brother, still live? Remove the Hedjet White Crown from the head of Heru and cast him into the waters, that I may contend with him regarding the office of the Ruler."

Amun-Ra considered Set's words, and he ordered the Hedjet White Crown to be removed from Heru's head. Then

Set taunted Heru, saying "Let us change ourselves into hip-popotamuses and plunge into the waters to fight this out. Whichever of us emerges from the water within the next three months shall not be made King of the Two Lands."

Seeing no other option, Heru changed his form into a hippopotamus and chased Set, in his hippopotamus form, into the waters.

Aset sat weeping on the shore, and she cried aloud, "Set has killed my son Heru!"

She then took a quantity of yarn and made a cord, and a she melted down a pound of copper into a barb, which she tied to her rope. She threw the barb into the water in the exact place where Heru and Set had plunged into it. The barb stung her son, Heru, and he cried aloud, "Come unto me, my mother Aset! Call to your barb to release me—I am Heru, the son of Aset!"

And Aset called out to the barb, "Loosen yourself from him; behold, he is my son Heru, my child."

And her barb loosened itself from him. Then Aset threw her barb into the water again, and it bit into Set. "What have I done against you, my sister Aset? Call to your barb and loosen it from me, for I am your brother on the side of the mother, O Aset," Set cried out.

Then Aset felt great compassion for her brother, as Set called to her saying "Do you desire enmity against your brother on the side of the mother?"

Aset ordered her barb to release Set, saying: "Loosen from him; behold, it is the brother of Aset on the side of the mother into whom you have bitten."

And the barb loosened itself from Set.

Heru grew angry and his face became savage like a panther. He removed the head of Aset with his great sword and placed her head on his chest. Then he ascended the mountain.

Thereupon, Aset changed herself into a statue with no head. Amun-Ra asked Tehuti, "Who is this female that has come, and she has no head?"

And Tehuti replied, "O my good lord, this is Aset, the mighty, the god's mother, and her son Heru has removed her head."

Amun-Ra cried aloud in horror, saying to the Council, "Let us go and inflict great punishment upon Heru."

Amun-Ra replaced the head of Aset with a cow's head, and the Council ascended the mountain to search for her son, Heru.

SET TAKES HERU'S EYES

VEN as the Great Council of the Gods searched for Heru in the mountains, he was far away in the Oasis country. Set found Heru lying under a Shensuha tree.

Upon seeing him, Set took hold of Heru, removed his eyes from their sockets, and buried them under the mountain to illuminate the earth. Heru's eyes became bulbs that grew into lotuses. Then Set returned and lied to Amun-Ra, saying, "I did not find Heru."

Thereupon, Hathor, lady of the southern sycamore, ventured forth and found Heru weeping in the Deshret. Hathor spoke to Heru, saying, "Open your eye, that I may put this milk in it."

When Heru opened his eye, Hathor poured gazelle's milk into the place where his eyes had been. She poured milk into his right eye and she poured it into his left eye; then she told him to open his eyes. As he opened his eyes, he found them restored. Hathor then left Heru and returned to Amun-Ra, telling him "I found Heru and Set had deprived him of his eyes. So, I raised him up again, and behold he has come."

The Council then said "Let Heru and Set be summoned so that we may judge between them."

And Heru and Set were brought before the Council. Amun-Ra addressed both Heru and Set, saying, "Go forth and listen to what I have said. Eat and drink, and let us be at peace. Cease this wrangling thus every day."

With that, Set spoke to Heru, and he said "Come, let us pass a peaceful day in my house."

And Heru replied, "I will do so, truly, I will do so."

In the evening, the bed was spread for them and they laid down. And in the night, Set caused his member to become stiff, and he made it go between the loins of Heru. But Heru put his hands between his loins and he caught the seed of Set. Then Heru went to speak to his mother Aset, "Come unto me, O Aset! Come and see this which Set has done to me!"

When he opened his hand, Aset could see the seed of Set. She cried aloud and seized her knife, which she used to cut off Heru's hand. She threw the hand into the water and fashioned for him a new hand of like worth.

Aset then ordered Heru to stiffen and expel his seed into a pot. The next morning, Aset carried the seed of Heru to the garden of Set. Aset questioned Set's gardener, asking him, "What herb does Set prefer to eat?"

And the gardener responded, "He eats no herbs from here, other than the lettuces."

Aset then placed the seed of Heru on the lettuce leaves. Just as expected, Set came to the garden and ate his lettuces, and he became impregnated with the seed of Heru.

Then Set spoke to Heru, and said to him "Come, let us go, that I may contend with you in the tribunal."

And Heru replied, "I will do so, truly, I will do so."

When the two arrived at the tribunal, the Council said to them, "Speak concerning yourselves."

Set responded: "Let the office of Ruler be granted to me. As for Heru, who stands before you here, I have performed doughty deeds of war against him."

Upon hearing this, the Council cried out loud, belching and spitting before the face of Heru. This caused Heru to laugh at them, and he swore an oath, "All that Set has said is false. Let the seed of Set be summoned, and we shall see from where it answers. Then let my own be summoned, that we may see from where it answers."

Tehuti, the lord of divine words, placed his hand upon the Heru's arm, and he said, "Come forth, seed of Set!"

And Set's seed responded from deep within the waters of the river where Aset had thrown it.

Then Tehuti placed his hand upon the arm of Set, saying, "Come forth, seed of Heru!"

And the seed spoke to him from within the depths of Set's stomach: "From where shall I come?"

Tehuti commanded it: "Come forth from the ear!"

The seed of Heru replied, "Shall I come from the ear, I who am a divine effluence?"

Then Tehuti ordered the seed of Heru to come forth from Set's forehead, and it came forth as a golden sun upon the head of Set. Growing extremely angry, Set stretched out his hand to grab the sun of gold, but Tehuti took it from him and placed it as an ornament upon his own head.

The Council then proclaimed, "Heru is in the right and Set is in the wrong."

47

THE GREAT BOAT RACE

ECAUSE of all his failures in his contests with Heru, Set realized he needed a better plan. When the Council of Gods declared Heru the winner of the latest contest, Set swore a great oath to the tribunal: "You shall not give the office to Heru, until he has been cast forth with me. We will fashion for ourselves some boats of stone and we will sail around. Whoever prevails in this race shall be given the office of Ruler."

Heru set about fashioning himself a boat of cedar, but he plastered it with gypsum. When Set saw the gypsum-coated hull of Heru's boat, he thought it was fashioned of stone.

So Heru went up the mountain, cut off its peak, and fashioned for himself a boat made of stone. Then the two contestants boarded their boats in the presence of the Council. Set's boat sank as soon as it was cast upon the water.

Angrily, Set changed his form into a hippopotamus and attacked Heru's boat. Heru quickly took his barb and threw it at Set, but the Council intervened, saying "Do not throw your barb at him."

So Heru took his weapons, placed them in his ship, and sailed down to Sais to speak to Neith, the mighty mother of gods.

THE COUNCIL CONSULTS AUSAR

ONG and hard did Heru fight with Set; but after Set's antics at the great boat race, Heru set sail to speak with Neith, the mighty mother of gods.

When he arrived, Heru pleaded with Neith: "Let judgement finally be pronounced upon me and Set. We have been in the tribunal for eighty years and none know how to pronounce judgement upon us. He has not scored a single victory against me, but a thousand times every day have I beaten him; and he disregards everything the Great Council has decreed.

"I fought him in the Hall of Two Truths and I was declared champion. I fought him in the Hall Heru-Prominent-of-Horns and I won. I fought him in the Hall Field-of-Reeds and I was the winner. I fought him again in the Hall The-Field-Pool and I scored a decisive victory against him."

The Council spoke to Shu, god of air, saying "Heru, the son of Aset, is right in all that he has said."

Tehuti then said to Amun-Ra, "Let a letter be sent to Ausar, that he may pronounce judgement on Heru and Set."

Shu then proclaimed: "That which Tehuti has said to the Council is right, a million times right."

Amun-Ra considered Tehuti's words and he ordered that a letter be written to Ausar asking for his judgement in the matter of Heru and Set.

Upon receiving the letter, Ausar quickly responded with a letter of his own. In his letter, the god of the underworld expressed anger that his son was being defrauded. He reminded the Council of the Gods that it was he who made the barley and grains that nourished the gods and all living creatures.

Ausar's letter was carried back to Amun-Ra, who sent a response back to Ausar, saying: "If you had never been born, the barley and grains would still exist."

Amun-Ra's response was read to Ausar, and Ausar sent back a threat to the Creator God: He would unleash all the demons and evil spirits of the underworld, the "savage-faced messengers who fear not man nor god", to murder the wicked in heaven and earth if Heru was not granted his rightful office.

When the Council heard Ausar's final response to Amun-Ra, they said "Ausar is the god of abundance and lord of plenty; and he is right in all that he has said."

THE FINAL CONTEST

N O one could argue against Heru's victory, especially after Ausar's sternly worded rebuke was read to the Council of the Gods.

Set quickly said: "Let us go again to Island-in-the-Middle, that I may contend with Heru there."

And the Council of the Gods went to Island-in-the-Middle, where they declared Heru the victor yet again.

At that point, Amun-Ra called upon Geb, god of the earth, to pass judgement on the quarreling princes.

Geb came before the assembled gods and addressed Heru and Set, saying: "Why do you quarrel amongst yourselves? You destroy the lands and hurt none but your subjects with every battle."

And Set and Heru were both unable to argue against the great earth god Geb, when he commanded them to cease their hostilities at once, lest they should face his wrath.

Geb then decreed that Set should rule over the place he was born, Upper Kemet, while Heru would rule over the place in which his father was drowned, Lower Kemet. He issued his command with the words: "I have separated you."

And, at long last, there was peace over the Two Lands.

And the Council of the Gods pondered the earth god's words and made inquiries of Geb. "Do you think they will be able to maintain peace with the Two Lands separated?" asked Anhur, the god of war.

"Do you not think it is wrong to deny the son of your first-born son the office of his father, as ruler of the Two Lands?" Tehuti inquired.

"Do we dispense justice by rewarding one who murdered his own brother?" asked Ma'at, goddess of justice.

As the tribunal questioned Geb's rulings, he carefully considered each point that was raised. After a while, Geb saw the wisdom of the tribunal and it seemed wrong to him that Set should receive a portion like to the portion given Heru.

So Geb reversed his ruling: "I hereby appoint Heru, the firstborn. Heru alone shall receive the inheritance of the Throne of Two Lands. Heru, the firstborn, shall henceforth be known as the Opener-of-Ways and Uniter of the Two Lands.

"And as for Set," Geb continued, "his only throne shall be as ruler over the barren lands of the Deshret. The murderer of his own brother, my first-born son, shall not be granted rule over the fertile lands nor their inhabitants."

Angered, Set rose up to deny the ruling of Geb, but Amun-Ra ordered Aset to silence him with her magic and to "bring him here, and fasten him with bonds."

Aset brought Set before Amun-Ra, fastened with bonds, as her prisoner.

Amun-Ra then spoke to Set, saying: "Who are you that you defy judgement upon yourself, yet you have stolen the Throne of the Two Lands from Heru?"

Set spoke up for himself, saying "Not so, my good lord! Let Heru, the son of Aset, be given the throne of his father Ausar."

Heru then stood before the Council, they set the Hedjet White Crown upon his head, and he was raised to the place of his father, Ausar. And the Great Council of the Gods spoke to Heru, saying, "You are the Good King; our hearts rejoice that you enlighten the earth with your comeliness."

Thereupon, Ptah the great, south of his wall, said: "What is that which shall be done with Set? For now, behold, Heru has been raised to the place of his father Ausar."

And Amun-Ra said, "Let Set, the son of Nut, be given to me, that he may dwell with me and be as my son. He shall thunder in the sky and men shall fear him."

The Council responded to the Creator God, saying "Heru, the son of Aset, is arisen as Ruler!"

Amun-Ra replied to them in kind: "Jubilations! All bow before Heru, the son of Aset!"

Aset then said: "Heru is arisen as Ruler, the Great Council is in celebration, heaven rejoices!"

The entire earth rejoiced when they saw Heru, the son of Aset, finally ascend to the throne of his father Ausar.

THE RESURRECTION OF AUSAR

ERU ascended to the throne of his father, and reed and papyrus were placed on the double door of the House of Ptah to signify Heru and Set, pacified and united.

The two princes fraternized and ceased their quarreling in whatever place they happened to be. Being united in the House of Ptah, the "Balance of the Two Lands", in which Upper and Lower Kemet had been weighed.

Aset and Nebet-Het then went forth to the burial chamber of Ausar in the House of Sokar without delay, for Ausar had drowned in his water. Aset and Nebet-Het looked out, beheld Ausar, and attended to him. Heru spoke to the goddesses, saying "Hurry, grasp him, prevent him from drowning!"

And the sister goddesses heeded the words of Heru in time and brought Ausar to land, while saying: "We come, we take you with us!"

Ausar entered the hidden portals in the glory of the lords of eternity, in the glory of him who rises on the horizon, on the ways of Amun-Ra of the Great Throne. He entered the palace and joined the gods of Ptah, the lord of years.

At the command of Geb, a royal fortress was built to the north of the land, and Ausar came into the earth at the royal fortress. Heru arose as king of Upper and Lower Kemet, in the embrace of his father Ausar and of the gods in front of him and behind him.